For Tammy

- K

Tater & Chip Go to the Beach
Copyright 2017 by Mabela Press
Written by Kari Litscher DeBruin
Illustrated by Ros Webb

All rights reserved. No portion of this book may be reproduced, stored in a retrieval system or transmitted in any form or by any means—electronic, mechanical, photocopy, recording, scanning or other—except for brief quotations in critical review or articles, without the prior written permission of the publisher.

Published in Oskaloosa, Iowa by Mabela Press. Mabela Press is an imprint of Mabela Press.

ISBN: 978-0-9981307-3-6

Tater & Chip Go to the Beach

Written by

Kari Litscher DeBruin

Illustrated by

Ros Webb

Mabela Press

I AM SO EXCITED!!

Today, my family is going to the beach!!
I LOVE the beach! I look beach-ready, right?

"Tater!? Do you have your sunscreen?"

"Yes, Mom."

"Do you have your swimsuit on? Are your beach toys packed?"

"Yes!... and Yes!" Moms sure ask a lot of questions!

"Do you want Chip to come?"

Do I want Chip to come?

Now THAT is a tough one. Chip is my dog. I love him, but he can be trouble. And, I mean TROUBLE. He doesn't mean to be. It's just his nature, I guess.

I think really hard.

"Yes!" I decide.

The car ride is SO fun. Chip is hanging out the window – his face looks crazy! My mom is trying to talk to us but no one is listening.

My brothers are scream-singing their songs and I'm thinking about the AMAZING sandcastle that I'm going to build.

I can NOT wait to get there!

"We're here!" I shout as I jump out of my seat, and run to the water. The boys and I jump off the dock. Chip barks his head off.

But, where's Mom? Oh there she is! She's carrying everything down from the car. She's so strong!

It's time to get busy building!
I scoop, pat, and dump.
Scoop! Pat! Dump!
I need water!
I need a stick!

This. Is. Awesome.
This is going to be my very best sandcastle EVER!!

My sandcastle ↓

Bucket + Spade ↓

I am in sandcastle heaven!

This is the biggest, most awesome-est sandcastle I have ever built. I am SURE if they gave awards for sandcastles, I would most definitely win them ALL.

For Real!

The only thing left for me to do, is to FILL my moat.

This is a seriously big moat. So, I seriously need help. I ask my brothers to help me. My oldest brother says no. He's too busy talking to girls...he's always talking to girls. But, my other brother says he'll help! Yes!

We grab the biggest bucket, scoop up the hugest wave and turn back to fill the moat and...

My brother tries to help me fix it, but it's too late.

Ruined. Totally, totally ruined.

I start to cry. My mom and my brothers say things to me, but I can't hear them. I'm bawling my eyes out. I'm so mad. I'm so sad.

Mom says it's time to go home.

The ride home is NOT fun. Mom is trying to talk to us. My brothers are trying to sleep.

Chip is hanging his head out the window. I'm quiet now, but my tears keep sneaking out.

A big truck passes us and scares Chip.

He lets out a gigantic "YELP!" and jumps into my lap.

I'm still mad at him. But when I see his scared little face, I feel sorry for him. For a little while, we just stare at each other. Then, he starts to lick away my tears.

He smiles his big goofy smile. I smile too.

"This dog is TROUBLE" I say, and I wrap my arms around his hairy, sandy neck. "But I LOVE him."

Besides, what's a Tater without a Chip?

I LOVE CHIP

More Kari Litscher DeBruin books for you to love:

Dear Princess

When you are the daughter of the King you are a real Princess! Your Father in Heaven loves you very much and has written you a beautiful love poem telling you just how special you are!

Beautifully written and illustrated for precious princesses everywhere!

Tater's Valentine Surprise

Tater plans to make this her best Valentine's Day ever. It will take a lot of courage...can she do it?

Or does Mom have an even bigger surprise planned?

www.ingramcontent.com/pod-product-compliance
Lightning Source LLC
Chambersburg PA
CBHW040331300426
44113CB00020B/2728